Public Health *for Kids*

Public Health *for Kids*

First Edition

Daniel A. Teoli

All rights reserved. No part of the material protected by this copyright may be reproduced or utilized in any form or by any means, electronic or mechanical, including photocopying, recording or by any information storage and retrieval system, without written permission.

Copyright © 2010 by Daniel A. Teoli
This edition published by Cherry Falls Publishing.

ISBN 978-0-9832356-0-6

First Printing (December 2010)
Authored by Daniel A. Teoli
Edited by Robin Teoli

Cherry Falls Publishing
A division of Brenum Books, Inc.
Los Angeles, CA 90014.

Printed and bound in the United States of America

Daniel D. Teoli, Sr.
Thank you for showing me that for any job it is only a matter of using the right tools.

&

Mary R. Teoli
Thank you for sincerely being "my biggest fan".

TABLE OF CONTENTS

Introduction...1

Part 1 – What is Public Health?..7
    Section 1: A Bright Idea...9
    Section 2: Epidemiology..15
    Section 3: Environmental Health................................21
    Section 4: Nutrition..27
    Section 5: Behavioral Science...................................33
    Section 6: Occupational Health.................................41
    Section 7: Biostatistics..47

Part 2 – I, Me, My...53
    Section 1: Simple Physiology....................................55
    Section 2: Body Mass Index (BMI).............................67
    Section 3: Physical Activities....................................71

Part 3 – Good Habits, Strong Futures..................................75
    Section 1: Personal Hygiene.....................................77
    Section 2: Washing Your Hands................................83
    Section 3: Wear Shoes Outside.................................89
    Section 4: Dental Care and You.................................97
    Section 5: Eye Care and Vision................................103
    Section 6: All About Sleep......................................111

Part 4 – What's Cookin'?..119
    Section 1: A Healthy Balanced Diet..........................121
    Section 2: Is Junk Food "Junk"?...............................127
    Section 3: Water...141

Conclusion..149

Answer Key..151

Introduction

 Whether you have already heard about the subject of public health or not, you are going to love this book!

Where else can you find all types of cool information about not only being healthy today, but making sure that you stay healthy tomorrow?

This book was written with a very simple and consistent structure which will allow you to skip around to the topics that interest you most.

Of course, I hope that you read and benefit from the entire book, but if you suddenly want to read about a specific topic (such as "Why do I need sleep?") - no problem!

If you are looking for a special section, all you have to do is look at the *Table of Contents* at the front of this book to find the page that you are looking for.

You will not have any problems with skipping around and starting new sections because each section is written to "stand alone" (which, for example, basically means that you will not have any trouble reading *Section 5* if you decided to skip *Section 4*).

Each section will follow a similar pattern: the name of the section and/or topic will be listed, a short hypothetical [pronounced: hi-poe-thet-ick-ull] situation (this is when we think about something that *could* happen, but maybe *hasn't* happened *yet*) may be written and then we will discuss the facts and details that you should know concerning the topic in relation to public health and/or your well-being.

You will notice that there is a short quiz at the end of each section. I bet that I know what you are thinking right now:

"DRATS! I don't like taking quizzes. I have to study for quizzes in school and they are no fun at all!"

Well, guess what?

I did not always like taking quizzes in school either! So I have tried to make the quizzes in this book *different* than the type that you have to take at school (you may even be surprised that these quizzes are fun!).

I know that you are really smart and will not need to study for these quizzes, but if you ever need any hints you can always flip back to the section text if you need to reread any information. The quizzes will be a mix of Multiple Choice, True/False and Short Answer questions.

You can check your answers with the answer key at the end of this book (see page 151).

Keep an eye open for this little guy with the sign (above); he will let you know when a quiz is around the corner!

Introduction Quiz:

1. What subject is this book about?

    a. Chemistry.

    b. Math.

    c. Public health.

    d. Physical education.

2. Who is this book for?

    a. My parents.

    b. My teachers.

    c. Me and other kids like me.

    d. My grandparents.

3. True/False:

You can skip to any section in this book and start reading from there without any problems.

4. What is the goal of this book?
    a. To help me be healthy now and stay healthy in the future.
    b. To make my backpack heavier.
    c. To help me understand the field of public health.
    d. Both answers "a" and "c" are correct!

5. What can you do if you don't know the answer to a quiz question?

_____
_____
_____
_____
_____

All right! You survived the first quiz.
I'll bet you did pretty well, too!

Part 1

What is Public Health?

Public Health For Kids

Tip: When your mother told you "not to talk to strangers"… She meant it.

Section 1.1: A Bright Idea

Public health is the active science of helping to improve and protect the well-being of people and the neighborhoods that they live in. Public health workers achieve this goal by researching and studying communities - just like yours!

The first task of most public health workers is to look at a group of random people from a neighborhood (or sometimes everyone in the neighborhood!) and see if they can spot any weird trends. If something sticks out as strange, the public health workers work hard to solve the problem.

Once the workers know the solution to the problem, they can start to develop education efforts to promote healthy changes for the citizens of that neighborhood.

Topics that may be of interest to the public health workers in big cities (and in your own hometown) might include:

- Disease and injury prevention
- Worker safety
- Environmental safety
- Diet recommendations

(We'll talk more about each of the "interests" listed above during later sections of this book.)

The field of public health is highly varied and is interested in many different "academic disciplines" (just like how your days at school are varied and have many different "academic disciplines" – like math, science and social studies).

However, instead of topics like math and social studies, public health is mostly interested in the following main areas:

- Epidemiology
- Environmental health
- Nutrition
- Behavioral science/Health education
- Occupational health
- Biostatistics

You can learn about each of these branches of public health in the remaining sections of *Part 1*.

Section 1.1 Quiz:

1. True/False:

Public health is the active science of helping to improve and protect the well-being of people (and their communities). _____

2. True/False:

Public health workers study communities by focusing only on *one single member* of that community. _____

3. Which of the following is a possible subject of interest to public health workers:

    a. Disease and injury prevention in a city.

    b. If it is going to rain tomorrow.

    c. How much you get paid to cut the grass.

    d. The favorite color of a community.

4. True/False:

Currently, there is only *one* discipline in the study of public health. _____

5. Describe the first task that is done by most public health workers:

_____
_____
_____
_____

Public Health For Kids

Section 1.2: Epidemiology

If you are like me, when you first saw the word written above on this page after "*Section 1.2*" you likely scratched your head.

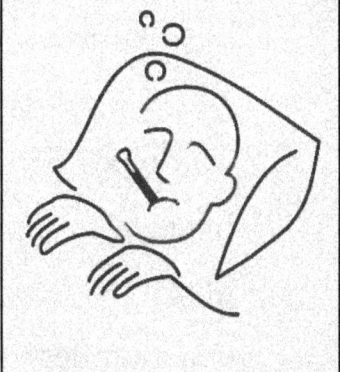

Epidemiologists are individuals that work in the field of epidemiology.

"What does that word mean? ...Epi-huh?"

That is exactly what I was thinking in my own head several years ago when I was first introduced to epidemiology [pronounced: epa-dee-me-all-o-jee].

15

However, luckily for us, to understand the core of the field is not as difficult as pronouncing its name.

Epidemiology is the study of diseases (or sickness) in large populations.

> Infectious diseases are things like the flu or the common cold – in other words, diseases that occur when small little critters like bacteria or viruses get into our bodies (and then increase in number while inside our bodies - which typically makes us feel sick).

The types of disease that are of interest to **epidemiologists** are pretty diverse – as are the communities that they study.

They may be interested in rare **infectious diseases** [pronounced: in-feck-shush] such as one that is affecting a community of people living in the jungle.

On the other hand, maybe they are interested in **chronic diseases** [pronounced: cron-ick] in your hometown...

Chronic diseases are things like diabetes or heart disease – in other words, diseases that are *not* necessarily caused by little critters getting into our bodies, but usually last for a very long time.

It really just depends on *when* you ask an epidemiologist as to what (and where) he or she is studying. In *Section 6: Biostatistics*, you can learn more about the techniques used in epidemiology.

Section 1.2 Quiz:

1. What causes infectious diseases?

    a. There is no cause for this type of disease, but it is long lasting.

    b. Getting sunburned.

    c. Not listening to our parents.

    d. Tiny organisms (or "critters") getting into our bodies.

2. True/False:
Epidemiologists often study diseases in large populations. _____

3. Which might an epidemiologist be interested in studying?

    a. A large population in New York City

    b. A large population in the jungle

    c. A large population in Alaska

    d. All of the above.

4. True/False:

Epidemiology is correctly pronounced as "Ep-ee-dam-all-gogy". _____

5. Describe what a chronic disease is and give an example:

_____
_____
_____
_____

Section 1.3: Environmental Health

The environmental health branch of public health studies shows how our environment affects our health and well-being. We will explore the field with the following example…

Hypothetical:

A lot of the people in Metro City are suddenly getting very sick. Also, the people are getting sick more often than they did in the past (for example, instead of only 100 people being sick at this time *last* year, now 800 people are sick *this* year).

After learning about the community and what sorts of activities the citizens do everyday, the public health workers notice a trend: almost all of the sick

people live in a certain part of town and almost all of the sick people drink unfiltered water from their sinks…

The public health workers find this pattern very interesting and wonder if the drinking water in that part of town is somehow related to the people getting sick.

The workers decide to go out and investigate where the drinking water is coming from (this is called doing *"field work"*).

The public health workers are surprised to find a giant crack in the water pipe which delivers the drinking water to the sick peoples' homes.

The workers also see that the large factory nearby is breaking the rules and polluting more than is allowed.

They discover that all sorts of dirt, bacteria and chemicals are getting into the water supply and this is what has been making most of these people sick in the community!

The public health workers notify the water company and the pipe is then fixed. Additionally, the workers notify the large factory that they are breaking environmental health rules and that they need to do a better job in the future.

The people in the community get better and the drinking water is now safe thanks to the hard work of the public health workers.

Section 1.3 Quiz:

1. In the story, what caused the sickness of most of the people in Metro City?

    a. A cracked water pipe.

    b. Bacteria getting into the water.

    c. Chemicals getting into the water from pollution.

    d. All of the above.

2. True/False:
Environmental health is the branch of public health that involves the study of where it is best to plant trees. _____

3. Which might an environmental health worker be interested in studying?

    a. The quality of water in a small town.

    b. The pollution levels of a new factory.

    c. Harmful gases that come from cars.

    d. All of the above.

4. Imagine that 115 people are sick at this time *next* year in Metro City (instead of the 800 people currently being sick in our hypothetical and with 100 people being sick last year). Do you think that it would cause panic or would it be somewhat normal for 115 people to be sick?

_____
_____
_____

5. Describe what "field work" is:

_____
_____
_____
_____

Section 1.4: Nutrition

When it comes to public health, the subject of nutrition is a very tasty topic. As you can imagine, a very important part of how we feel depends on what we eat and drink.

A **clinical setting** is a description of an area where medically related tasks are undertaken.

Examples of a location "in a clinical setting" would include your family doctor's office, a hospital, or other medical buildings.

Without going into great detail involving specific nutrients, we can still discover what exactly this branch involves; people that focus on this area often work hard to measure and test different diets in **clinical settings**.

Additionally, public health workers may develop and evaluate nutrition programs for middle and elementary schools, high schools and even colleges.

There are also areas within this topic that relate to more complex scientific functions (such as **metabolism** [pronounced: muh-tab-o-lizz-mmm]) and fields (such as **physiology** [pronounced: fizz-ee-all-o-gee]).

A simple way to think of <u>metabolism</u> is to consider it as to total sum of all chemical activities (or reactions) that take place in your body.

<u>Physiology</u> is a branch of science that involves the functions of living beings.

One of the other areas of interest to public health is research involving eating behaviors and problems.

For example, perhaps someone always wants to eat too much or maybe someone else wants to eat too little.

The public health workers try to figure out ways to treat these sorts of problems and even prevent them in the future by identifying risk factors.

What does the term "risk factors" mean? It is easy to explain the meaning of risk factors with a simple example about hair loss…

If you looked at a random group of 1,000 individuals that experience hair loss and found out that 950 of those individuals happened to be men and all 1,000 of the individuals were over the age of 30, you could identify two "risk factors for hair loss":
1) Being a man.
2) Being over the age of 30.

Section 1.4 Quiz:

1. Which is an example of a clinical setting?

　　a. A classroom.

　　b. A garage.

　　c. A hospital.

　　d. A sport stadium.

2. True/False:

The nutritional branch of public health can often involve metabolism and physiology. _____

3. Which organizations might benefit from nutritional programs backed by public health?

　　a. Colleges.

　　b. High schools.

　　c. Jails.

　　d. All of the above.

4. True/False:

Nutrition is *not* a very important branch of public health. _____

5. What are a couple examples of eating problems that relate to the nutritional branch of public health?

_____
_____
_____
_____
_____

Section 1.5: Behavioral Science

Behavioral [pronounced: bee-hay-v-yur-ul] science is a very interesting area of public health. You may not believe me right now, but I bet that you will change your mind by the end of this section.

Let's see if you can guess what this topic is all about by reading the following hypothetical:

Jimmy is a man that works for the behavioral science branch of the Metro City Public Health Department. Jimmy's main job for the next few weeks is to explore seat belt usage in Metro City.

He wants to find the answer to several very important questions: How many people wear their seat belt when driving in a car? How many people do not wear their seat belt when driving in a car?

A **statistic** is a number that explains or describes a group of people (in our example, the statistic of "45%" describes how many people are not wearing their seat belt).

…And the most important question: *Why* isn't *everyone* wearing their seat belt?

Jimmy picks out 100 people from Metro City and asks them about their "behavior" when it comes to wearing seat belts.

Jimmy finds that in Metro City 45% (or 45 people out of 100 people) are not wearing their seat belt when driving. The number (45%) is called a **statistic** [pronounced: sta-tis-tick].

The sign above is an example of the tools used to change behavior for a certain activity.

The next thing that Jimmy needs to do is focus on his main goal: he needs to figure out a way to make everyone want to wear their seat belt! But how will he do that?

Important Note:

Behavioral science can involve almost any behavior that you can think of – from riding a bike with a helmet to brushing your teeth for longer than one minute.

The answer is a simple one: since Jimmy already knows what the problem is and how they are not using seat belts…

He now needs to figure out what causes that behavior.

After asking a bunch of people why they do not wear their seat belt, almost all of them reply that they do not wear their seat belt because they forget to put it on when they get into their cars and do not think about it while driving.

So Jimmy devises a plan to help people remember to wear their seat belts in Metro City. He makes a bunch of commercials to play on TV reminding people to buckle up.

Also the Public Health Department puts up big billboards all across town saying:

"Buckle Up – It's the Law!"

A month later, Jimmy asks another 100 people from Metro City about their seat belt usage. Now only 8% of people do not wear their belt – which is much better than the 45% from before!

Section 1.5 Quiz:

1. Which is an example of a statistic?

    a. An apple is a fruit.

    b. Jack likes to play football.

    c. 80% of people say that they like apples.

    d. Jill bought milk because it was on sale.

2. True/False:

Behavioral science could involve finding out how many people in Metro City eat without washing their hands. Afterwards, they could then try to figure out a way to get more people to wash their hands before eating in the future.

_____

3. True/False:

In the example, Jimmy failed because 8% of people were still not wearing their seat belts at the end of the story. _____

4. After Jimmy found out how many people were not wearing their seat belts, what did he do next?

      a. Find out why people were not wearing their belts.

      b. Read a book about automobile safety.

      c. Started to make traffic signs.

      d. All of the above.

5. Can you think of your own example of behavioral science in action?

_____

_____

_____

_____

Section 1.6: Occupational Health

Occupational health [pronounced: awk-you-pay-shin-ul health] is the branch of public health that involves creating safe work environments and making sure that the employees (also known as workers) stay safe while doing their jobs.

When you think of the definition above, what sorts of jobs pop into your mind? You may think about construction workers moving heavy pipes around or maybe firefighters saving people from burning buildings – both of those examples would be correct!

Occupational health workers do sometimes focus on construction sites and the construction equipment. To keep the area safe, the occupational health workers set rules to make sure that objects do not fall on an employee's head (note: that is why construction workers wear those hardhats) and also make sure that the bulldozers and wrecking balls will not hurt anyone.

The firefighters have a similar relationship with the occupational health workers. As you can imagine, when firefighters run into a burning  building, they are exposed to a lot of smoke and other chemicals which can really hurt their lungs.

An example of how occupational health relates to firefighting is that they make sure that the firefighters have special gas masks that protect firefighters' lungs as much as possible.

You may be wondering if these are the only jobs that occupational health is involved with and the answer is: no way! Almost every job that you can think of has been affected by the rules and concerns of occupational health...

A worker that types on a computer all day may have a special pad for his wrists on the keyboard (this is an example of **"ergonomics"** [pronounced: urr-go-nah-micks]).

Ergonomics is the study of designing a workplace so it is safe for the worker's physical health (for example, avoiding backaches by using good chairs or stopping knee pain by standing on special rubber mats).

Have you ever had to get an x-ray? Do you remember what the person that took your x-ray did right before they pushed the button? They probably left the room or went behind some type of shield.

You may have seen the pad attached to a keyboard (like the one right above) – it is an example of occupational health in action!

This is also an example of occupational health. The x-ray workers need to be careful not to be too close to the x-ray machine because they may get sick (remember they take x-rays for people *all* day long – so the amount of x-rays that their bodies would be absorbing would build up over time… kind of like how my friend Billy Bob's stamp collection built up over time, but that is a story for another day!)

Public Health For Kids

Section 1.6 Quiz:

1. Which is an example of occupational health in action?

    a. Firefighters using special gas masks to protect their lungs.

    b. A teacher eating a golden delicious apple.

    c. Police officers wearing blue colored shoelaces.

    d. A librarian reading a book.

2. True/False:

Ergonomics involves designing a workplace in order to maximize worker safety and physical well-being. _____

4. True/False:

Almost all jobs have been affected by occupational health in some way or another.

_____

4. Which might benefit from learning more about occupational health?

    a. A construction worker.

    b. An x-ray technician (worker).

    c. A firefighter.

    d. All of the above.

5. Can you think of any other jobs that may have been affected by occupational health issues? How so?

_____
_____
_____
_____

Section 1.7: Biostatistics

The name may look funny, but biostatistics [pronounced: bye-oh-sta-tis-ticks] is a very serious part of public health. (Note: Biostatistics is the combination of the words "biology" and "statistics".)

Biostatistics is all about finding trends (or patterns). When you think of trends/patterns, you may first think about zigzagging lines that you drew during art class, or maybe how the seasons follow a trend during the year (summer, fall, winter, and spring).

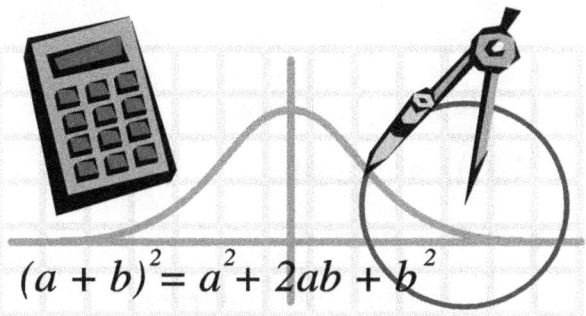

Another example of a trend are the following words as shown: "blue, red, white, blue, red, white, blue, red, white, blue, red…"

Can you see the trend? What color would come next after "red"? The answer: white!

The examples above are similar to what we mean when talking about "trends" in biostatistics. However, the trends usually are much harder to find! Very rarely will the trend pop right out such as in our example of "What color comes next?"

So what can these **biostaticians** [pronounced: bye-oh-sta-tish-anns] do since the trends are too hard to see with their eyes alone? The answer for this branch of public health is to use numbers and math concepts in order to "spot the trend".

Biostatiscians are people what work in the field of Biostatistics.

(The man above is a good example of how hard these guys work to spot trends, but today they often use special computer programs to help instead of regular old calculators.)

A simple hypothetical:

Bobby, the biostatician, is working on figuring out if there is a trend between working 12 hours a day and hair loss in men.

The first thing that Bobby does is gather all the information he will need in order to "spot the trend." In this case, it is asking 1,000 men about how much they work and also about their own hair loss.

After gathering all of the answers from the men, Bobby begins to analyze [pronounced: an-ul-ize] the data (which basically means that he is studying the answers he got back from the men).

> **Important Note:**
>
> Biostatistics often has a very close bond with the field of epidemiology (we talked more about that in Section 1.2).
>
> In other words, when someone is working in one of those fields, they usually use tools/methods from the other field as well.

Bobby finds that 500 out of the 1,000 men have hair loss (50%). Furthermore, he finds out that *out of those 500 men with hair loss*, 490 of them work over 12 hours a day. Bobby has spotted the trend! He might then notify the occupational health workers that if men work longer and longer hours, they may lose more and more of their hair!

Section 1.7 Quiz:

1. What do biostaticians use to help spot trends?

    a. A magnifying glass.

    b. Computer programs about the alphabet.

    c. Special computer programs to "analyze the data".

    d. None of the above. Biostaticians do not spot trends.

2. True/False:

Bobby was successful in his goal of spotting a trend. _____

3. Which is an example of a trend similar to the one in our hypothetical?

    a. Yellow, blue, blue, yellow, rabbit, green.

    b. 1, 2, 3, 4, 1, 2, 4, 6.

    c. 90% of people eat pizza while sitting.

    d. There are 26 letters in the alphabet.

4. True/False:

Biostatistics and epidemiology are tied together closely within public health. _____

5. Can you think of any other trends that may be of interest to biostaticians?

_____
_____
_____
_____
_____

Public Health For Kids

Part 2

I, Me, My…

Tip: Do you know the telephone numbers for your local emergency departments (the fire department, police station, etc.)? Don't forget 9-1-1!

Section 2.1: Simple Physiology

 Physiology [pronounced: fizz-ee-all-o-jee] is a branch of science that focuses on how and why living things work (or "function").

When we say "how and why living things function" you may first think about how you, or your friend, or maybe even how a frog functions – and you would be correct! All of the previous examples are living things (also known as "organisms").

However, physiology goes deeper than just focusing on the entire organism as a whole. In fact, they divide up living organisms into little neat packages (or "systems").

Among the many systems that are studied, some that you may have heard about include:
- The nervous system
- The circulatory system
- The respiratory system
- The immune system
- The musculoskeletal system

Let's take a moment to talk about each one of these common systems…

A) The nervous system

The nervous system is what makes you, well, you! If you think about it (which, by the way, will require the use of your nervous system), you can understand what I meant after answering a couple of quick questions…

If you dyed your hair the color blue, would you still be yourself? Of course, you would just have blue hair.

If you made your voice sound really deep or really squeaky, would you still be yourself? Sure, you would just sound different.

When a sick person gets a new heart at the hospital,

are they the same person even after getting a different heart in their body (note: this is called a "heart transplant")? Even if this happens, you would still be "you".

What if someone got an entirely new brain? That person wouldn't have any of the same memories, thoughts or feelings like before. You wouldn't recognize your parents, teachers or friends. If that happened, you would be a different person!

The brain is a major part of the nervous system, with something called a "spinal cord" also being part of the system. (You may think the word "spinal" looks a lot like the word "spine" [or backbone] and you would be correct if so! The spinal cord is located all along the inside of your backbone. The spinal cord helps your brain "talk" with other parts of your body.

The nervous system is responsible for giving you the five senses and also giving you the ability to do things like laugh, see, smile, smell, cry, sing, dance and think.

B) The circulatory system

The circulatory [pronounced: sir-Q-la-torry] system involves how your blood is pumped throughout your body. Blood may not sound very fun at all – most likely whenever you see your own blood it's when you fall off your bike or trip on the sidewalk. But your blood is a very important piece of you.

All over the inside of you – from the top of your head, to your fingertips, to the bottom of your toes – there are little tunnels running throughout your body. Some of these tunnels are bigger than others and some pump blood in different directions (either toward your heart or away from your heart).

In fact there are three main different types of tunnels that your blood travels in throughout your body:

1) *Veins* – these are like big busy highways that carry blood back *towards* your heart.

2) *Arteries* – these are like busy highways that carry blood *away* from your heart.

3) *Capillaries* – these are like skinny little streets and alleys that carry your blood all over the place… Well, ALMOST all over the place. Things like your hair and fingernails do not have any working capillaries inside them.

Without your blood you wouldn't be able to live very long. The air that we breathe is processed in a special way by our lungs and the air provides us with "oxygen" [pronounced: ox-ee-jin], which is absorbed into our blood.

The blood flows throughout our entire body, delivering the fresh oxygen and helping our bodies run properly. This brings us to…

C) The respiratory system

The respiratory [pronounced: ress-per-a-torry] system involves all the parts of your body that play a part in breathing (or "respiration").

The [simplified] typical path that air travels for us to complete respiration goes something like this:

Nose ⟹ Pharynx ⟹ Trachea ⟹ Lungs
          ["fair-nix"]   ["tray-key-ah"]

Once the air is received into the lungs, oxygen is passed through many (and I mean a ton) of tiny little structures called *alveoli* [pronounced: al-vee-oh-lie], The alveoli are responsible for putting the fresh oxygen into our blood. They are like mini "air sacs" or balloons that fill up with the air that we breathe. Then the oxygen goes through and into our blood and travels throughout our bodies. Amazing, huh?

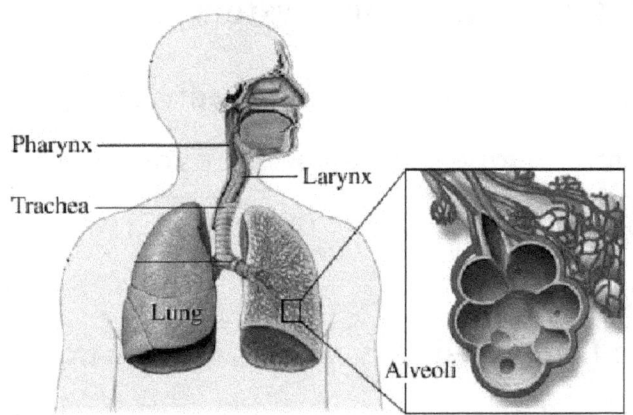

D) The immune system

The immune [pronounced: e-mm-you-nn] system is made up of many types of special cells that are kind of like security guards.

When germs and other bad things get into our bodies, it is our immune system that kicks into gear and saves the day.

Without going into too many complex details, the special immune system cells have a way of knowing which bad guys to look out for (kind of like the "wanted" posters in cowboy movies). When the immune system cells cross paths with a germ that matches the "wanted" poster, it attacks and stops the evil-doer in its tracks. In other words, it knocks it out and destroys it!

E) The musculoskeletal system

The musculoskeletal [pronounced: muss-cue-low-skel-e-tal] system is made up of both our skeleton (bones) and our muscles.

With the joint effort of both our skeleton and muscles working hard, we can enjoy movement (such as walking), support (so we can stand tall) and form (without a musculoskeletal system, we would just look like a pile of weird jelly).

Section 2.1 Quiz:

1. What is the purpose of the musculoskeletal system?

    a. Support.

    b. Form.

    c. Movement.

    d. All of the above.

2. True/False:

The immune system is responsible for being the security guard inside our bodies. _____

3. What is the purpose of having veins?

    a. Veins have no purpose.

    b. Veins carry blood back towards the heart.

    c. Veins carry blood away from the heart.

    d. All of the above.

4. True/False:

Physiology is the study of how living organisms function. _____

5. What are some of the important functions of the nervous system?

_____

_____

_____

Section 2.2: Body Mass Index

You may have heard adults talking about Body Mass Index (or BMI for short) or maybe you heard it mentioned on television... But what exactly is it?

Well, let's start by saying that it is a very important measurement and that everyone (even you) has one.

BMI is simply a calculation of how much body fat a person has by using not only someone's weight (like bathroom scales do) but also the person's height!

If a person has too much fat tissue on their body it is not good for their health. However, if an individual has *too little* fat on their body it isn't healthy either.

Public Health For Kids

(Above) An example of what a BMI Chart looks like.

There are charts in some textbooks [as well as calculators on the internet] which can tell you your BMI, but the best option is to see your family doctor for a reading. Your doctor will be able to accurately explain the results in order to let you know how you "measure up".

Section 2.2 Quiz:

1. What does BMI stand for?

    a. Body Mass Imaging.

    b. Big Mass Index.

    c. Body Mix Index.

    d. Body Mass Index.

2. True/False:

Having too much or too little fat on your body can be unhealthy. _____

3. Which of the following is the best person to ask about your BMI?

    a. My friends.

    b. My doctor.

    c. My dentist.

    d. My teacher.

4. True/False:

Everyone has a BMI (including me).

_____

5. Do you think that the BMI is a perfect system? Why or why not?

_____

_____

_____

Section 2.3: Physical Activities

Kids do not always like to do what is good for them. Not many kids like to eat their brussels sprouts at dinner or go to bed early for a full night's sleep.

Often kids do not like to wear their safety gear while riding bikes or rollerblading because they think it is not very "cool".

However, one thing that kids do like to do [which is also good for them] is to go outside and play.

When you go outside and have fun, you are exercising without even trying!

Riding your bike, playing tag and football or even having a snowball fight are all types of exercise. During each of these physical activities, not only are you having a blast, but you are also making yourself healthier by building up a strong body.

So what are some specific benefits of being active?
- Your muscles get stronger and bigger.
- Your joints get (and stay) flexible.
- Your heart is strong and healthy.
- Your bodyweight remains in a healthy range.
- You just feel great!

What are some ideas? Jump rope, basketball, dancing, football, soccer, tumbling, gymnastics, running, hiking, hopscotch, kickball, climbing trees, cheering, wrestling, water balloon fights, building snow forts, swimming, and many more – they are all great ways to stay healthy!

Section 2.3 Quiz:

1. What are the benefits of physical activity?

    a. Stronger muscles.

    b. More flexible.

    c. You feel great.

    d. All of the above.

2. True/False:
Playing and being active is only good to do during the summer time. _____

3. How is your heart affected by physical activity?

    a. It is not affected.

    b. It gets weaker.

    c. It gets stronger.

    d. None of the above.

4. True/False:
Kids don't always like to do what is good for them. _____

5. Can you think of any other fun activities that you could do for physical exercise?

_____

_____

_____

_____

_____

Public Health For Kids

Part 3

Good Habits, Strong Futures…

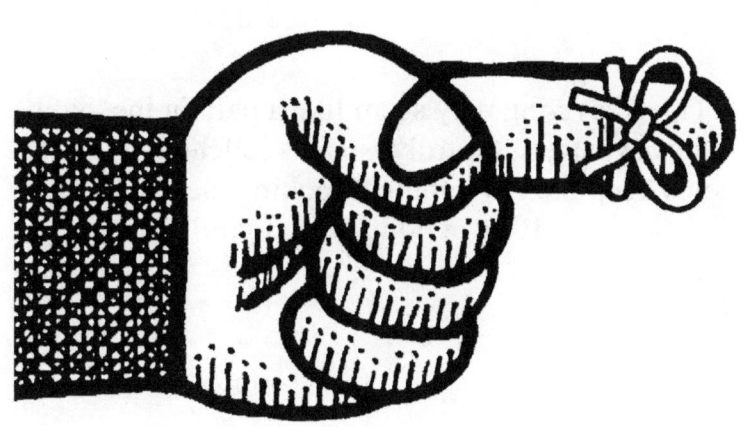

Tip: Recycling may seem like a pain in the "you-know-what", but it truly is an excellent activity that helps keep the environment looking clean and lively. If I can do it, so can you!

Section 3.1: Personal Hygiene

 At one point or another, you likely heard your mom, dad, teacher, or friend mention the phrase: personal "hygiene" [pronounced: hi-jean].

Hygiene is a funny looking word that simply means "doing some action that will help to keep your body staying healthy".

So when you hear someone say, "You need to have good personal hygiene," they are basically saying that you need to do certain activities that will keep your body happy and healthy.

From the definition above, you may first think that good personal hygiene is referring to doing physical activities and sports (like we talked about in *Section 2.3*) – and if so, nice work! You are very smart to apply what you learned before to the new topics that we are talking about now. However, having good personal hygiene is just *a little* different than doing physical activities and playing outside…

Having good personal hygiene refers to what you do *after* you are finished playing.

"Huh? What do you mean? I don't do anything after I am done playing outside because then I'm just too darn tired!"

If you are thinking something like the above idea then you are a good thinker! But take a moment to think a little bit further…

Public Health For Kids

What types of activities do you do *after* you are done playing outside all day in the middle of the hot summer?

"Well, I go back home, get something to drink and eat dinner. Then I shower to get all the dirt and sweat off my body…"

BINGO!

Having good hygiene means that you made it a habit to do the activities that keeps your body healthy – in a "fresh, clean, nice smelling" sort of way.

When you take a shower (or bath) after you play

outside, you are not only cleaning all the sweat and stinky smells off your skin, but you are also washing off a bunch of nasty bacteria – bacteria that can sometimes make you sick!

Some of the other ways of having good personal hygiene are:
- Washing your hands before you eat.
- Wearing shoes when you go outside.
- Brushing and flossing your teeth.

Each of the three points listed above are so important, that they have their own special sections in this book. You can read all about them in the next several pages.

Section 3.1 Quiz:

1. What are the benefits of having good hygiene?

   a. It helps me stay healthy.

   b. It helps me stay clean.

   c. All of the above.

2. True/False:

The word "hygiene" is correctly pronounced like "hay-gee-knee". _____

3. Which is an example of good personal hygiene?

   a. Walking the neighbor's dog.

   b. Washing the neighbor's dog.

   c. Taking a shower after walking and washing the neighbor's dog.

   d. None of the above

4. True/False:

Good personal hygiene happens all by itself. I do not need to do anything to have good personal hygiene._____

5. Can you think of any other ways of having good personal hygiene which were not mentioned in this section?

_____
_____
_____
_____
_____

Section 3.2: Washing Your Hands

 This section holds the super secret way to help keep you safe from nasty things like the flu and colds and germs. What is the secret? You guessed it: Washing your hands!

You use your hands to do so many different things:

- Open doors
- Close doors
- Play sports
- Write papers
- Wrestle with friends
- Change your little brother's diaper
- Read books
- Shake hands
- Text messaging

...You get the idea.

Many people think that they only need to wash their hands before they eat, but people can get the flu from just scratching their nose, rubbing their eyes or touching their mouth! When you rubbed your eyes during that baseball game last week, you might have  helped the flu germs get into your body. Those little flu critters are pretty tricky, huh?

Do you wash your hands correctly?

I will describe the way you should wash them and you tell me if you have been doing it correctly or not. Ready?

Turn the water on warm and wet your hands. Grab the soap (or liquid soap) and get your hands completely covered in a thick layer of bubbles (this is called "lathering up").

Once your hands are all nice and soapy, rub them together and make sure you get the front and back of your hands as well as between your fingers. If you have long fingernails, you really want to clean under those nails. Your wrists likely have some nasty critters on them also, so it is a good idea to get them all soapy too.

You should do this for at least 20 seconds (an easy way to measure how long 20 seconds is to slowly count backwards from 20 down to 0 or you can sing "Happy Birthday" to yourself three times).

After that, you are all set! Wash off all the soap and grab the nearest clean towel to dry up! Look at those hands: Clean as a whistle!

So what do you say? Have you been washing your hands *correctly*?

If you have been doing it correctly, great – keep up the good work! But if not, no problem, just follow the directions above.

Because it is so important to clean your hands, it is worth mentioning (one more time) to wash:
- Before you rub your eyes or touch your nose or mouth.
- Before eating or handling food.
- After you blow your nose in tissues or sneeze into your hands.
- After coughing on your hands.
- After playing outside.
- And, of course, after using the restroom.

Section 3.2 Quiz:

1. Why is washing your hands a good idea?

    a. It helps keep me from getting sick.

    b. It helps stop me from spreading germs.

    c. It helps me have good personal hygiene.

    d. All of the above.

2. True/False:

To correctly wash your hands all you need to do is rub them under water for 10 seconds.

_____

3. What are some activities that can cause you to get germs on your hands?

    a. Playing sports.

    b. Shaking hands with a neighbor.

    c. Using the restroom.

    d. All of the above.

4. True/False:

It is important to clean under your fingernails when washing your hands._____

5. What are some other activities that you did today that you should wash your hands after doing?

_____
_____
_____
_____
_____

Section 3.3: Wear Shoes Outside

 When it comes to shoes, there are all types: wide shoes, thin shoes, long shoes, short shoes, dark shoes, light shoes, tennis shoes, dress shoes, summer shoes, winter shoes, and on and on…

The important part is not what type of shoes you wear as much as it is that you just wear some shoes. Period.

It may be funny trying to picture someone going to school without any shoes on and I agree – that would be very weird.

However, a lot of people like to walk around barefoot outside (whether it is in the park, in a locker room, in their backyard during barbeques or even just to their mailbox to grab the mail!

The problem is that by walking around without shoes on, you are exposing your poor feet to all sorts of dangers.

Just like what we talked about regarding washing your hands in *Section 3.2* (because they get germs all over them from the things that we do all day) your feet get bad germs and viruses on them from walking around barefoot.

You may even get a wart on your foot! (If you don't know what a wart looks like just think about the bumps on a witch's nose – those are warts.) It is important to say that getting a wart on your foot is not super bad. You can either go to a special doctor that can remove the wart or your parents may be able to buy some special stuff at the store that removes warts.

Neither option feels good. In fact, both downright hurt! So, if you can avoid getting warts on your feet by wearing your shoes: good choice!

Another risk from not wearing shoes is that you do not always know what you are going to step on. You may think that the grass at the park is nice, soft and springy – but what about that broken piece of glass hidden in the grass? Ouch!

Your backyard has to be safe! Right? There is no broken glass back there… But what about other dangerous things like thorns, sharp stones, or nails? When workers build houses it is common for some stuff (like nails) to fall out of their pockets and into the grass. If you happen to step on it…Again, ouch!

When people go to the public community pool during the summer to cool off, they often have to shower first before jumping into the water. Many people think that the showers have to be clean (I mean, how can it be dirty? It is a shower!). But the truth is that it is very, very bad to walk around in the public showers (and locker rooms) without shoes (or sandals) on. Without having something protecting your feet, you may catch something called "Athlete's foot" (which is when your feet itch and burn constantly – no fun at all!).

Now you know the best choice for you (and your super important feet) is to stay protected from the risks that you can't always see.

With shoes on (even if it is just a pair of summer sandals), the germs, glass, and nails will have no chance of ruining your (or your feet's) day.

Section 3.3 Quiz:

1. Why is it important to wear shoes outside?

    a. It protects me from sharp things like glass.

    b. It protects me from things I can't see.

    c. It protects me from bad germs.

    d. All of the above.

2. True/False:

If you are just walking around in your front yard playing, it is not important to wear shoes.

_____

3. Which of the following is a safe place to walk around without shoes on?

    a. The shopping mall.

    b. The school locker room.

    c. The parking lot.

    d. None of the above.

4. True/False:

It is more important to have on a pair of shoes than the type of shoes that you are wearing.

_____

5. Can you think of any times or places where it is safe to not wear shoes on your feet?

_____

_____

_____

_____

Section 3.4: Dental Care and You

 Caring for your teeth (or "dental care") can be such a hassle. Every night you have to drag yourself into the bathroom when you are tired and brush each tooth, making sure that you covered all the dimples in your molars… And then you have to floss. (You do floss, right? *Right?*)

While it may seem like a pain, it will be a much bigger pain for you if you decide to stop brushing and flossing your teeth (and the people who are around you will not be happy either due to your bad breath!).

When we brush our teeth, we prevent dental "cavities" [pronounced: cav-it-ee's] from developing. What causes cavities is the build up of plaque [pronounced: puh-lack] on and around our teeth.

What is this "plaque"? Well, it is basically just tons and tons of little bacteria having a good old time sticking to our teeth. When we enjoy food and drinks that have a lot of sugar in them, the bacteria get really excited and eat some of the sugar themselves.

The problem is that when the bacteria eat the sugar, they digest it and produce stuff which slowly eats up your teeth (this is called tooth "decay" [pronounced: de-kay]).

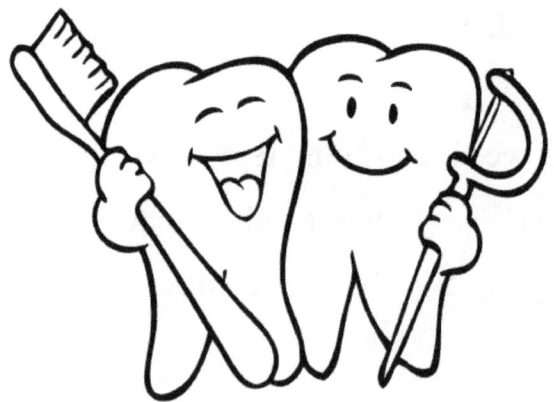

The best way to stop these bacteria from hurting our teeth is to brush at least twice a day with toothpaste and to also floss once a day (because that cleans *between* our teeth where the toothbrush cannot reach).

Hey, it is important to mention that taking care of our teeth also makes us have fresh breath. You know how your mouth  tastes yucky in the morning? Well, when you brush, you are cleaning away all the bacteria and smelly stuff that leaves your mouth clean, smelling nice, and ready to start the day.

Make sure that you brush all your teeth (not just the easy ones in the front!) and that you also take your time. I remember when I was a kid my friend used to brag that he could brush his teeth in under

10 seconds. Now, he doesn't have hardly any teeth left to brush!

For tips on exactly how to brush and floss your teeth, ask your family dentist or one of your parents to show you extra slowly.

Dentists aren't scary people.

I have never met a dentist that I did not like and I bet that you will not meet one that you do not like either. I agree that they can be a little scary sometimes, but they are just trying to keep us healthy with a nice, white smile and clean, fresh breath…Which all of your friends will be happy about!

Section 3.4 Quiz:

1. What is dental plaque?

    a. An award you win at school.

    b. Food stuck to your teeth.

    c. Bacteria stuck to your teeth.

    d. All of the above.

2. True/False:

You only need to see your family dentist once every two years. _____

3. Which of the following is the main benefit of flossing?

    a. It sounds cool.

    b. It is fun trying to reach the back teeth.

    c. It cleans where toothbrushes cannot reach.

    d. None of the above.

4. True/False:

Brushing your teeth is the only way to get fresh smelling breath – flossing your teeth does not matter. _____

5. What are some specific foods that you think may be more likely to cause cavities in your teeth?

_____

_____

_____

_____

_____

Section 3.5: Eye Care and Vision

 I do not need to tell you how important your eyes are. You already know that your eyes help you with almost every task that you do – both indoors and outdoors.

When I was in school, a teacher gave us a simple homework assignment to complete that night: Each of us was told to blindfold ourselves in our own bedroom for a period of an hour. We were to do all the normal activities that we would usually do. Then we were to write a little paper on what we learned.

Well, I found out that it is a lot harder to do anything without using my vision [pronounced: viz-zun]. I "saw" how important it was to take care of my eyes from that moment on.

So how can we take care of our eyes? Well, the good news is that it is pretty easy to do! The largest risk to our eyes is summed up in one simple word: strain.

Have you ever been sitting in class and had to squint your eyes really hard to see the chalkboard? Or maybe when you were riding in a car, have you had to look really hard to read that sign that is passing by?

If so, you may be straining and it is not making your eyes happy. In fact, if you strain your eyes all the time, it may give you nasty headaches or even make your vision worse!

I bet you already know what the solution is… Eyeglasses and contact lenses come to mind.

Why do some people need to wear glasses while other people don't need them?

Well, when you hear someone say that "everyone is different, special and unique" they are not lying. Everyone's vision is different!

So it makes sense that, while the classmate on your right does not have any trouble reading the homework assignment written on the chalkboard, your classmate on the left can barely read the words.

If you are a lucky student with 20/20 vision (that means that you can see almost perfectly) then you don't need to worry about wearing glasses. But, if you are like me, then your eyes are a little tired and you need help seeing clearly, so you wear glasses.

There are two main types of vision problems among students in school:

- *Nearsighted* people can see things clearly up close, but have trouble seeing things far away (like a chalkboard at the other end of the classroom).

- *Farsighted* people can see things clearly far away, but have trouble seeing things close up (like the words in the textbook on their desk).

If you think that you may have one of the problems outlined above, ask your mom or dad to take you to the eye doctor. After the doctor completes a couple of simple tests, she will know what type of problem you have and can help you. And then comes the fun part...

Picking out your glasses!

When picking out a pair of glasses it can be really fun. Do you like thick frames or thin frames? Do you want dark or bright frames? Heck, some glasses don't even have frames! It is really up to you! (Just make sure that they are "fitted" correctly. I once had a really cool pair of glasses, but they always slid down my nose because I did not take the time to have them fitted correctly!)

Section 3.5 Quiz:

1. What does vision involve?

    a. Winter hats.

    b. Eyesight.

    c. Your ears.

    d. All of the above.

2. True/False:

Everyone has different eyes and thus different eyesight. _____

3. What does farsighted mean?

    a. A person can see things clearly far away.

    b. A person can see things clearly close up.

    c. A person can see clearly at all distances.

    d. None of the above.

4. True/False:

If someone has 20/20 vision this means that they can see very well. _____

5. Other than headaches, can you think of any other risks from not wearing eyeglasses if you should be wearing them for your eyes?

_____
_____
_____
_____
_____

Section 3.6: All About Sleep

Take a moment to think about all the stuff you did yesterday. You may have gone to school, did you homework, played with friends, helped your mom or dad around the house, maybe you even cut the grass. It is a lot for anyone to do, but even if you do not feel sleepy after doing all of those things, two things that are ready for a little break are your brain and your body.

You may think that you give your body and brain rest when you sit down at night and watch television or play on the internet. I mean it is not as hard of a task as doing math

homework or taking out the trash, right? Right…

However, the only activity that truly provides your body and brain with a break is when you sleep.

Sleep is kind of like cleaning your room. After a while your room gets messy, clothes are on the floor, stuff is out of place, new toys are in the corner. But when you clean your room, everything gets put in order and is neat. You know where everything is and if your mom tells you to find your red shirt, you know exactly where to find it.

The above example is just like what happens when you go to sleep. Your brain is full of all sorts of new information that you learned during the day (whether it is what you learned at school or what you learned watching television, reading, talking to friends or surfing the internet).

By sleeping, you allow your brain to "clean its room". Everything is put in order and your brain will be able to quickly locate information when needed (such as where you put that red shirt).

If you are between the ages of 8-12 you should try to get around 10 hours of sleep per night. If you can get 10 hours of sleep each night, then you will be fresh and ready to tackle any task that your brain does the next day.

When you do not get the sleep that you need, strange things start to happen. You are more likely to get angry and sad, you may yell at your friends without having any reason. You may also start to do poorly in school because you cannot concentrate that well anymore. I heard a story about a famous basketball player that once lost a game because he did not sleep the night before the game. He played really poorly and his team was not very happy with his decision to stay up all night. Another very good reason to get the sleep you need is that, if you do not, it may slow down your growth!

If you need some tips on how to get the best sleep you can, check out these ideas:

- Try to skip any drinks that contain something called "caffeine" in it. This ingredient gives people little boosts of energy, which is fine during the day – but not a good thing before trying to go to sleep.

- Try to relax before you lie down, read a book, watch a quiet television program or take a warm bath. (Whew, I'm getting sleepy myself just thinking about it!)

- Try to use your bed only for sleeping (not as a seat for eating, watching television, playing video games, etc.) It may sound silly, but by only using your bed for sleeping, your body and brain will know that it is time for bed every time you climb on it.

- Try not to do anything that gets you too worked up, excited or scared before bedtime (for example watching a scary movie).

Section 3.6 Quiz:

1. What should you use your bed for?

    a. To lie on while watching television during the day.

    b. A seat while talking to friends on the phone.

    c. Only for sleeping.

    d. All of the above.

2. True/False:

Kids only need about 6-8 hours of sleep per night.

_____

3. Which movie would be best to watch before bed?

    a. An exciting sports movie.

    b. A really funny movie.

    c. A super scary movie.

    d. None of the above.

4. True/False:

Drinks with caffeine are very good for helping people fall asleep during the night.

_____

5. Do you have a bedtime routine (in other words, do you do the same set of activities every night before going to bed)? If so, what is your routine?

_____
_____
_____
_____
_____

Public Health For Kids

Part 4

What's Cookin'?

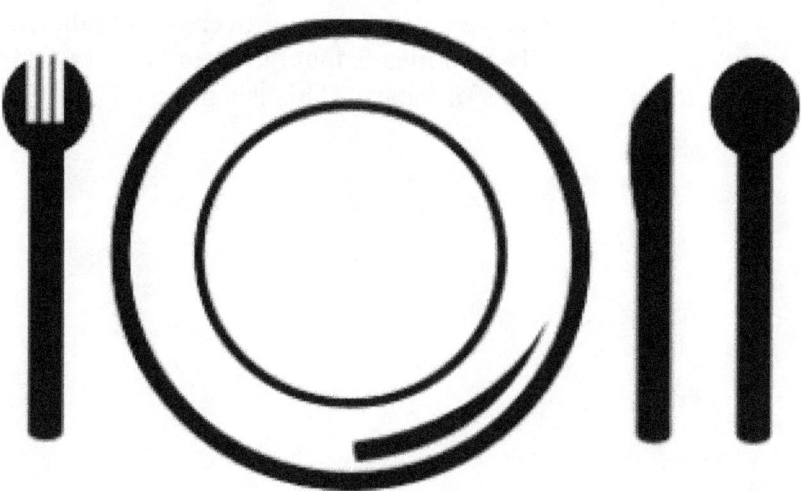

Tip: Have you ever seen meat at the grocery store labeled as "lean"? Typically lean means that the meat has less fat in it than other cuts of meat… This is a good thing!

Section 4.1: A Healthy Balanced Diet

As you learned in *Section 1.4* nutrition plays a major role in the field of public health. Some people spend their entire career focusing just on what foods are best for us to eat!

However, it is not just those mysterious public health workers that are interested in a healthy balanced diet – but you should be, too.

Not only do we feel better when we have the right kind of diet, but it is extra important for kids because you are still growing. When kids are on a healthy balanced diet, their growth can be like a rocket… It just takes off!

So what exactly is a healthy balanced diet?

Well, it is best explained with the help of a simple picture: a food pyramid.

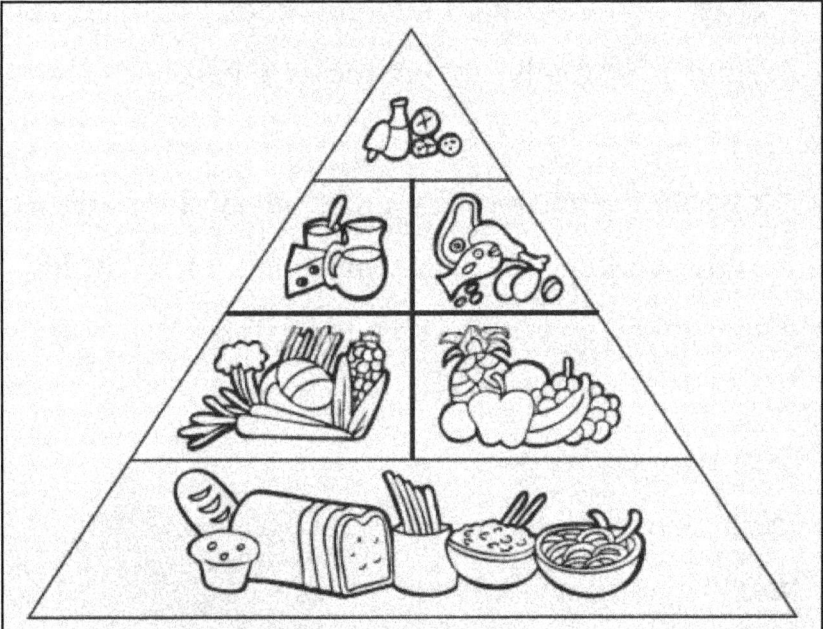

A food pyramid is designed so that the foods at the *big* bottom should be a *big* part of our diet and the foods at the *little* top should be eaten just a *little*.

Concerning how much of each level you should eat each day – well, that depends on a few different things…like your age, your weight, and if you are a boy or a girl.

Our public health friends recommend that growing kids should eat the following amount of each food group per day:

- Grains and Bread: 6 ounces
- Fruits: 12 ounces
- Vegetables: 20 ounces
- Milk and Dairy: 24 ounces
- Meats: 5 ounces
- Sweets, Oils and Other Goodies: there are no set rules for junk food, but just a little bit (every now and then) will not hurt you.

The goal is to eat at least some of each food group each day. If the amount of each group that you eat does not exactly match the guidelines above, do not worry too much. They are simply guidelines to guide you to a healthy diet. However, if for some reason you had to skip eating one of the groups, the best group to skip is certainly the junk food category.

It is hard work changing your diet and it is extra hard if you really like what you eat now. But, if you need to change some groups around to match the healthy guidelines, try to do so slowly over a few days.

It is a lot harder to go from eating no vegetables one day to eating a bunch of vegetables the next day. The trick is to build up the amount slowly. Who knows, you might actually start to like eating your vegetables!

Section 4.1 Quiz:

1. What is a food pyramid?

    a. It is something built by the Egyptians.

    b. It shows the types of food that we should eat each day, as well as how much.

    c. It shows how much of a food is at the grocery store.

    d. All of the above.

2. True/False:

Kids should try to eat around 10 ounces of vegetables each and every day.

_____

3. True/False:

It doesn't matter how much junk food you eat each day as long as you have 20 ounces of meat.

_____

4. True/False:

Public health workers are interested in developing things like the food pyramid to help communities figure out their nutritional needs.

_____

5. Think about what you had to eat yesterday. How did it measure up to the food pyramid guidelines? Does anything need to be changed about your diet?

_____

_____

_____

_____

_____

Section 4.2: Is Junk Food "Junk"?

In *Section 4.1* we talked a lot about the importance of a balanced diet and exactly what "balanced" means.

In this section, we are going to discuss something that everyone loves to eat, but almost nobody likes to talk about. Any guesses? I'll give you a huge hint: the answer is in the title of this section.

Junk food. How can something that tastes so good be something that is so bad for our bodies?

The answer to that simple question is not so simple after all. In fact, there have been enough books written about junk food that you could probably fill an entire library with just those books. (So you know it is a bunch!)

While we will not go into so much detail that it will fill up an entire book, we will take a couple minutes to relax and chat about why these "comfort foods" are so uncomfortable to talk about.

The thing to remember is that it is not the food item itself that is bad, but rather it is the stuff that is put into making the item (also known as the "ingredients"). For example, a pizza could be really healthy or it could be really bad for you – it just depends on the ingredients. Below are three of the major bad guys when it comes to why junk food is "junk".

1) SUGAR

Sugar is just wonderful, isn't it? It makes our cupcakes taste sweet, our ice cream yummy… Darn it, it even gives us a little energy after eating our favorite candy bar after school. However, as my grandpa always said "there is another side to the coin". Sugar is no different – it tastes great, but there is another side to that chocolate coin.

When we eat sugary foods, it is true that they taste sweet. However, it is also true that they make the natural bacteria in our mouths go crazy (and I mean crazzzzy!). If you want to learn about why the bacteria go crazy for sugar, check out *Section 3.4* in this book. The main idea though is that eating foods with a lot of sugar in them are more likely to give us cavities…and NO ONE likes to get cavities.

Eating a lot of sugar can also have other bad effects on our bodies. In fact, remember how we just mentioned how eating that candy bar after school gave us energy? Well, that is not 100% true. While it may give you energy for a short period of time, you soon start to get really tired – and feel kind of like a slug. This is called a "sugar crash". Without getting into the heavy science behind what causes this "crash" to occur, just know that it is caused by our body responding to the large amount of sugar we just ate, and we get really tirrrrred. (Yawn…)

Not exactly something to look forward to, huh?

2) SALT

Some people love salt... Just love the stuff. Have you ever went to a restaurant to eat and noticed the guy that orders french fries and uses almost an entire salt shaker on one serving?

Who can blame him? Salt makes almost everything taste better, right?

While there are no right or wrong answers to the questions above (maybe some people do think that everything tastes better with salt), one thing that is clear is that foods that have a lot of salt in them (salt in food is also known as "sodium") can have a lot of undesirable effects inside the human body.

One of the main problems with consuming a lot of salt in your diet is that water really likes salt. How about a simple (and silly) example of how these two things interact within our bodies:

Let's pretend for a couple minutes that there were two people: one person was named "Salt" and the other person was named "Water". (Let's just ignore the fact that these two people would have pretty strange names!) Water is very much in love with Salt. In fact, Water wants to go everywhere that Salt goes and stay very close. As a matter of fact, once Water is around Salt it just will not leave until Salt finally leaves too…

Now applying the previous strange example to our bodies, can you figure out one of the main reasons why it is not good to eat a lot of salt?

If you said that it is "because once we eat a lot of salt, then water wants to stay in our bodies", you would be correct!

"Holding water", "retaining water", "water weight"… They are all descriptions of what happens to our insides when we eat a lot of salt: our bodies hold more water.

So what? What is the problem with holding more water than we normally would?

Again, someone could write an entire book about the answer to the last question. However, the main problem that we want to focus on is that the salt does two things in particular: it makes us heavier (from all that extra water inside us) and it can raise our blood pressure (blood pressure is the pressure of the blood that is flowing through our circulation system – for a little review of the circulatory system, check out *Section 2.1* earlier in this book). High blood pressure can lead to heart disease!

It is important to mention that salt is not ALL bad. We need to have a little salt in our daily meals to keep us healthy. However the problem arises when things get unbalanced and we eat too much – it is all about balance.

3) FAT

Fats are the trickiest ingredient in junk food to talk about. Why? Because while there is, for example, only one type of "sodium" – there are a few different types of fats. But wait, it does not stop there. Some of the fats are actually good for us to eat!

There are three main types of fats that you will find in foods: unsaturated fats, saturated fats and trans fats.

Now the difference between these fats involves a science lesson that is a little too complex for this book. However, if you want to really get into the science, try asking one of your science teachers at school. They will be impressed by your curiosity. Believe me!

The important fact to remember is that the healthy ("good") fat is called unsaturated fat. While, on the other hand, the unhealthy ("bad") fats are called saturated fats and trans fats.

Public Health For Kids

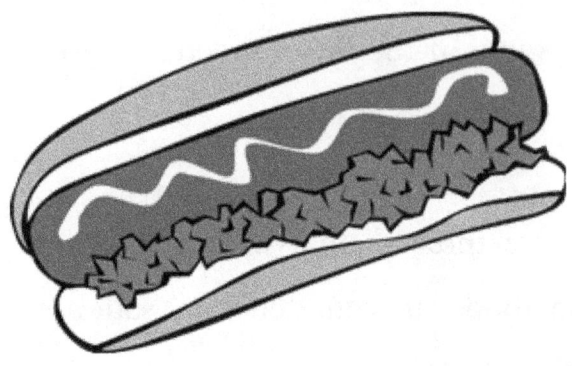

Food products that contain saturated fats include: cheese, fatty meats and butter. Margarine and cake frosting are examples of food items that contain trans fats.

You can find unsaturated fats in things like: fish, olive oil and nuts.

Whew! We covered a lot in this section and I know there is a lot of material to "digest" (okay, it was a bad joke). But, truly, there are a lot of useful details that are important to know and understand.

As you progress through school you will likely learn more about the "science" behind what you should eat and what you should avoid.

For now – just recognizing what is good and bad (and what should be balanced) is a great start!

Section 4.2 Quiz:

1. What are the unhealthy types of fats often found in food?

    a. Trans fats.

    b. Saturated fats.

    c. Unsaturated fats.

    d. Both answers "a." and "b." are correct.

2. True/False:

Salt should be completely removed from our diets because it serves no purpose in our bodies.

_____

3. True/False:

Sugar is an excellent source of long-lasting energy, especially after a long day at school.

_____

4. Which is a bad effect from eating a lot of salt?

    a. It requires a lot of pepper.

    b. It can raise blood pressure.

    c. It can lead to loss of smell.

    d. None of the above.

5. Can you name three foods that are high and/or low in each of the three main ingredients we talked about in this section (i.e. sugar, salt and fat)?

_____

_____

_____

_____

_____

Section 4.3: Water

The subject of this section is so useful [and so important] to our lives each and every day, that the subject gets its own area in this book – and it even comes last (as they say, "save the best for last").

Water is, by all means, one of the most important things that we put into our bodies (well, second most important if you are considering the air we breathe). This fact may come as a shock to you – water is more important than food. Why is water so important?

You would be absolutely correct to feel that food is a very important part of our lives (you read all about why in *Sections 4.1* and *4.2*). However, did you know that the human body can live for 7-8 weeks without food? It would certainly not be a healthy practice. We should all eat a healthy balanced diet every single day. But the fact remains that we can live for almost 2 months without eating.

On the other hand, there is water. How long do you think a human can live without drinking any of this clear, refreshing liquid? 4 weeks? 2 weeks?

The correct answer is about 3 to 5 days. That's right – not even 1 week. Why is this? I mean there is not much to water really; it's just a clear liquid without a taste or a smell. (Well,

unless you buy flavored water, that is.)

The answer to why water is so important rests within ourselves. The human body is 60-75% water (depending on who you ask). That is a lot of water! But why do we need so much of it in our bodies?

Water performs countless tasks in every inch of us from head to toe. Some of these tasks include:

1) Water helps keep our eyes moist.
2) Water helps to keep our bone joints moving smoothly.
3) Water is a major part of the blood in our body and thus helps oxygen travel through our circulation system (see *Section 2.1*).
4) Water helps keep our body at a stable temperature of 98.6° F.

5) Water helps our body get rid of the bad wastes in our body (in other words, it helps us use the restroom).

6) Water keeps us hydrated [pronounced: hi-dray-tid].

Being "dehydrated" (the opposite of being hydrated) is dangerous because our body does not have enough water in it to do the things that it needs to do.

(For your own information, signs of being dehydrated include: being dizzy, having a dry mouth, having a fast beating heart… just overall feelings of "blaaah".)

So how much water should you drink every day? Most doctors and public health workers seem to recommend about 8 glasses of water each day. If it is really hot outside and you are playing sports, you may drink more. If you are just relaxing in your bedroom; you may need just a little less.

Water is the perfect subject to end this book with, because, not only is it one of the most important things needed to keep the human body working, but also it is a major interest in the field of public health.

Many public health workers test water to make sure it is safe to drink and try to figure out if the drinking water is making a community sick (like our example earlier about *environmental health* in *Section 1.3*).

With that said, go get yourself a tall glass of water, I would like to make a toast: "To you, to me and to public health. Cheers!"

Drink up!

Section 4.3 Quiz:

1. Why is water important to the human body?

   a. It keeps our eyes moist.

   b. It is good to fill the fish tank with.

   c. It helps our joints work smoothly.

   d. Both answers "a." and "c." are correct.

2. True/False:

We only need to drink about 3-4 glasses of water each day to keep our bodies healthy.

_____

3. True/False:

Water helps keep our body at a stable temperature of 75.8 ° F.

_____

4. What percentage of the human body is water?

    a. 25-30%.

    b. 35-45%.

    c. 60-75%.

    d. None of the above.

5. We mentioned that the example from *Section 1.3* tied the field of public health to the importance of water. Can you think of any similar stories that would tie the two topics together?

_____

_____

_____

_____

_____

Conclusion

You made it! Congratulations! We talked about a lot of different topics, systems, activities, jobs, foods and drinks. The one subject that ties them all together: the field of public health.

I hope you learned interesting facts from this book and I also hope that you share what you learned with at least one other person. (Of course, feel free to share with more people. You know how the saying goes: "the more the merrier".)

It has been a pleasure writing this book and maybe one day we will run into each other and have a nice, tall glass of water together. (And it will be clean water too – if public health workers have anything to say about it!)

Tip: "An apple a day keeps the doctor away"…but bananas and oranges cannot hurt either.

Answer Key:

Introduction Quiz:
1. C
2. C
3. True
4. D
5. Free answer: You can go back and look through the section material for the answer (or hints) to quiz questions.

Section 1.1 Quiz
1. True
2. False
3. A
4. False
5. Free answer: The first task of most public health workers is to look at a group of random people from a neighborhood (or sometimes everyone in the neighborhood!) and see if they can spot any weird trends.

Section 1.2 Quiz:
1. D
2. True
3. D
4. False

5. Free answer: Chronic diseases aren't directly caused by little critters getting into our bodies (those are more like infectious diseases); however, chronic diseases can be said to last a long time and stay with a person – like heart disease, diabetes, arthritis and cancer.

Section 1.3 Quiz:
1. D
2. False
3. D
4. Free answer: It would likely be somewhat normal. 115 is only 15 more people than the prior year's 100 people. 800 people is a very large jump compared to only 115.
5. Free answer: Field work is when a public health worker leaves the office and goes out to the location where they are interested in studying (it could be Antarctica, Africa or even your backyard).

Section 1.4 Quiz:
1. C
2. True
3. D
4. False
5. Free answer: Two problems that pertain to eating which may be of interest to public health are

people that "overeat" (eat too much) or "undereat" (eat too little).

Section 1.5 Quiz:
1. C
2. True
3. False
4. A
5. Free answer: Public health workers may be interested in studying such things such as why people start doing drugs or gamble, among countless other interests.

Section 1.6 Quiz:
1. A
2. True
3. True
4. D
5. Free answer: Truck drivers have been affected by occupational health matters. There are rules that many companies set for how long a driver can drive without going to sleep or taking a break – thus helping to keep both the driver and other people safe on the highways.

Section 1.7 Quiz:
1. C

2. True
3. C
4. True
5. Free answer: There are tons of trends that may be of interest to biostaticians. One example would be that 70% of people with a specific chronic disease smoke cigarettes. (Note: this is a made up trend, just to provide an example answer.)

Section 2.1 Quiz:
1. D
2. True
3. B
4. True
5. Free answer: The nervous system controls almost everything that occurs in the body in some way. It also helps the different parts of the body communicate with each other.

Section 2.2 Quiz:
1. D
2. True
3. B
4. True
5. Free answer: No, I don't think that the BMI is a perfect system. For example, some people with a high BMI may be almost all muscle, while a person with a low BMI may be all fat. So BMI doesn't take into consideration these issues.

Section 2.3 Quiz:
1. D
2. False
3. C
4. True
5. Free answer: I could go on a hike, play tennis, play football, go for a jog, walk a dog, swim at the pool, play lacrosse, etc.

Section 3.1 Quiz:
1. C
2. False
3. C
4. False
5. Free answer: One way to help keep good hygiene that was not mentioned in the section text is to keep your toenails trimmed. If they get too long, they could hurt your toes and they may get infected!

Section 3.2 Quiz:
1. D
2. False
3. D
4. True
5. Free answer: Today when I went to deliver a letter, I had to open a door and open the mail box. It was a good idea to wash my hands before eating lunch!

Section 3.3 Quiz:
1. D
2. False
3. D
4. True
5. Free answer: My friend named Mike never lets anyone wear shoes in his apartment. In fact, he doesn't wear shoes in the apartment either – just socks. Since all the floors are carpeted, it would likely be okay to walk around without shoes on since his carpets are clean and there are no sharp nails sticking out of the floor. Also Mike always cleans up any spills or messes right away, too. So there is no chance of stepping on a piece of broken glass either.

Section 3.4 Quiz:
1. C
2. False
3. C
4. False
5. Free answer: I think that sticky candy like taffy causes more cavities – because it has a lot of sugar in it and this type of candy is more likely to stick to teeth and cause plaque to build up.

Section 3.5 Quiz:
1. B
2. True

3. A
4. True
5. Free answer: If you are doing an activity like playing sports, you may not be able to see the ball and it may hit you on the head!

Section 3.6 Quiz:
1. C
2. False
3. D
4. False
5. Free answer: Yes, I do have a bedtime routine. I always read a chapter or two from one of my favorite books. Then I gave a small glass of water, brush my teeth, fluff my pillow and then go to sleep.

Section 4.1 Quiz:
1. B
2. False
3. False
4. True
5. Free answer: After thinking about what I ate yesterday, I don't think I had enough vegetables. I also had too much milk. I should change my diet by cutting back on milk and eating more vegetables!

Section 4.2 Quiz:
1. D
2. False
3. False
4. B
5. Free answer: Foods that are high in sugar would be candy. Foods that are low in sugar would be vegetables. Foods that are high in salt would be potato chips. Foods that are low in sodium would be fruits. Foods that are high in fat would be hamburgers. Foods that are low in fat would be skim milk or yogurt.

Section 4.3 Quiz:
1. D
2. False
3. False
4. C
5. Free answer: There could be a story about how the all the people in a small community [that eat fish from the same lake] got very sick. After studying the water in the lake, public health workers find that there are all sorts of dangerous chemicals in the water that are being absorbed by the fish – then the chemicals get into the people when they eat the fish!

Public Health For Kids

Notes:

Public Health For Kids

Notes:

Notes:

Public Health For Kids

Notes:

www.ingramcontent.com/pod-product-compliance
Lightning Source LLC
LaVergne TN
LVHW041623070426
835507LV00008B/416